The Art of Selling Art
From Art Studio to Marketplace

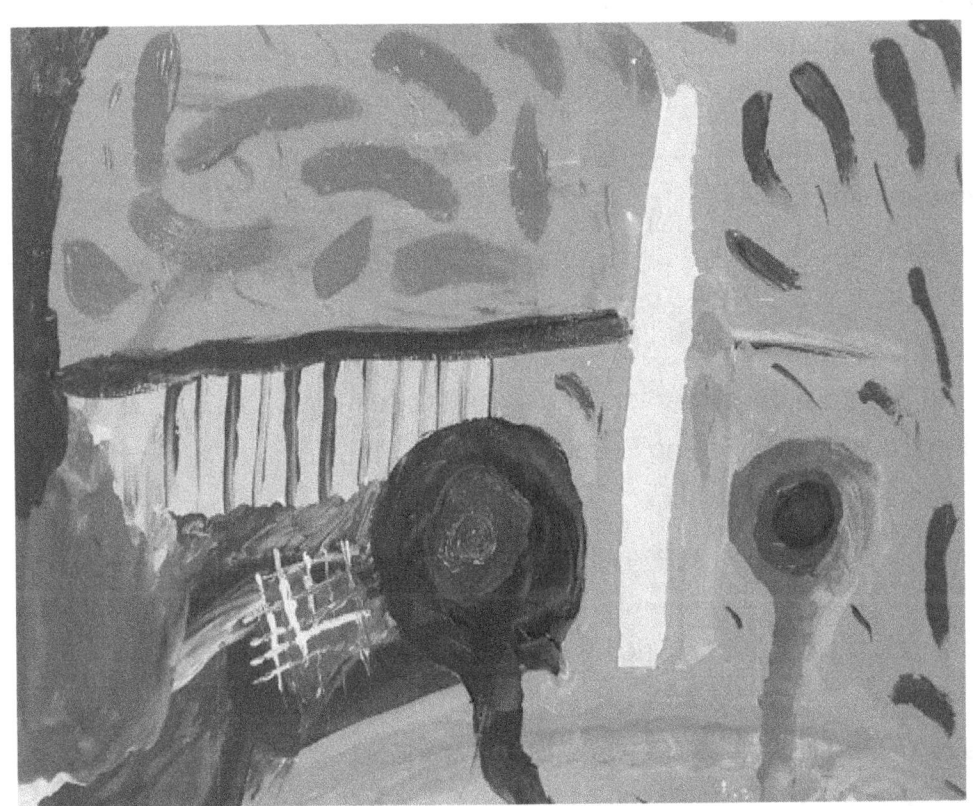

By

Aliyu Aminu Ahmed

Contents

The Art of Selling Art: From Art Studio to Marketplace

Introduction

By opening this book, I infer that you possess a fervent interest in art, or perhaps you identify as an artist yourself. If so, this book is crafted precisely with you in mind.

Welcome to a transformative journey that turns your deep passion for art into real economic rewards. The craft of selling art intertwines the imaginative spirit with the business world, requiring a blend of artistic flair and strategic thinking. This guide is crafted to guide artists through the intricate journey of creating, branding, marketing, and finally, selling their artwork. It acts as an extensive guidebook to traverse the intricate and sometimes overwhelming intricacies of the art world— that can seem formidable and maze-like to those just beginning to explore its depths.

Art, in its essence, is a profound reflection of the soul, a physical manifestation of the intangible. It embodies personal expression at its most visceral, yet the moment we decide to commercialize our art, it transitions into a product within the marketplace. This dichotomy underscores a truth many artists confront: the inherent personal connection to their creations. Initially, the thought of parting with one's art might seem anathema to the creative spirit. This reluctance is natural, stemming from the deeply personal nature of the creative process. However, as you continue to produce more work, the practical realities begin to surface—art materials such as paints, canvases, and other essentials accumulate costs. Additionally, what may have started in a corner of your living room or the confines of a basement soon outgrows these spaces, necessitating the consideration for a dedicated studio or perhaps even a gallery.

The reality is, sustaining your passion for art becomes increasingly challenging without the infusion of financial resources. It's at this juncture that the necessity to sell your art emerges—not merely as a choice but as a vital step towards continuing your artistic journey. Transitioning from an artist to an art entrepreneur encapsulates a myriad of challenges. It demands more than raw talent; it requires a mastery of skills often left unaddressed by traditional art education, including branding, marketing, sales, negotiation, and a comprehensive understanding of the digital landscape.

As we delve deeper into the subsequent pages, we will unearth the core principles underlying the sale of art. From deciphering your unique value proposition to forging meaningful connections with your target market, our objective is to unravel the complexities of this process. Through practical advice and actionable strategies, this book aspires to empower you with the confidence to adeptly navigate the art market. Embark on this journey with an open mind and a willingness to embrace the multifaceted role of an "artrepreneur", poised to transform your creative passion into a thriving, profitable venture.

Understanding Your Market

At the heart of selling art is the market—comprised of collectors, art enthusiasts, and casual buyers, each with their own tastes, needs, and budgets. Understanding this market is critical to successfully selling your art. Who are they? What do they want? And, perhaps most importantly, how can you reach them?

The art market is diverse, spanning local art fairs to global online platforms. Each segment offers different opportunities and challenges. Local art fairs, for example, provide a direct way to connect with buyers but may have a limited reach. Online platforms, on the other hand, can connect you with a global audience but require digital marketing savvy.

To navigate this landscape, you'll need to conduct market research. Start by identifying your ideal buyer. Are they seasoned collectors or people looking for a beautiful piece to decorate their home? What is their budget? What styles and themes do they prefer? Understanding these factors will help you tailor your marketing efforts and choose the right channels to reach your audience.

The Art Ecosystem

S/N	Who are they?	What do they want?	How can you reach them?
1	Artists	To create and sell art	Social media, personal websites, art shows
2	Collectors	To acquire and sometimes trade art	Art fairs, galleries, online platforms
3	Art Galleries	To exhibit and sell art, represent artists	Direct submissions, artist networks, online presence
4	Art Dealers and Advisors	To buy, sell, and advise on art transactions	Networking events, industry conferences, referrals
5	Auction Houses	To facilitate buying and selling of art via auctions	Auction house submissions, online listings
6	Museums and Cultural Institutions	To collect, preserve, exhibit, and educate about art	Exhibition proposals, cultural events, educational programs
7	Art Critics and Writers	To analyze, interpret, and review art	Press releases, art blogs, social media
8	Art Fairs and Festival Organizers	To bring together artists, galleries, collectors, and the public	Participation applications, art community engagement
9	Art Schools and Educational Institutions	To offer education and training to aspiring artists	Admissions, open days, educational fairs
10	Art Students	To learn and develop as future artists or art professionals	Art competitions, exhibitions, social media
11	Corporate Collectors	To invest in art for corporate collections	Corporate art consultants, direct proposals
12	Government and Cultural Policy Makers	To regulate, fund, and influence arts initiatives	Policy submissions, arts advocacy groups
13	Art Handlers and Transporters	To move and install art safely	Professional directories, art logistics forums
14	Art Conservators and Restorers	To preserve and restore art for future generations	Referrals, professional conservator networks
15	Insurance Companies	To provide insurance for art	Insurance brokers specializing in art, online inquiries
16	Art Investors and Investment Firms	To invest in art as a financial asset	Investment forums, art finance conferences
17	Digital Platforms and Online Marketplaces	To facilitate the online viewing, buying, and selling of art	Listing artwork, digital marketing strategies

| 18 | Art Therapists | To use art in therapeutic contexts | Professional associations, healthcare networks |
| 19 | Art Licensing Firms | To manage the rights for reproducing art on products or in media | Licensing trade shows, intellectual property lawyers |

Next, consider your positioning in the market. What makes your art unique? Is it your technique, your subject matter, or perhaps the story behind your work? This unique selling proposition (USP) is what sets you apart from the thousands of other artists vying for attention. Articulating your USP is crucial to attracting the right buyers to your work.

Finally, stay abreast of market trends. The art world is constantly evolving, with shifts in buyer preferences, the emergence of new selling platforms, and changes in the way art is consumed. Keeping an eye on these trends will help you adapt your strategy and stay relevant in a competitive market.

Moving Forward

As we delve deeper into the topics of marketing and selling art in the chapters that follow, remember that success requires more than just understanding the market. It demands perseverance, adaptability, and a willingness to learn and grow. Whether you're a seasoned artist looking to expand your reach or a newcomer to the art world, this book is designed to equip you with the knowledge and tools you need to thrive in the business of art.

Let's embark on this journey together, embracing the challenges and opportunities that lie ahead. By the end, you'll not only be better equipped to sell your art but also to appreciate the beauty of the process itself—the art of selling art.

Chapter 1

Building Your Foundation

If you are still reading this book, I am sure you are interested in art. However, beware, for art holds a seductive allure, an addiction born from the act of creating something new, something astounding. Art is where the boundaries of creation are limitless, blending the intoxicating freedom of imagination with the tangible world.

As you embark on this journey, understand that art is not just an expression of creativity but a profound exploration of your soul's hidden parts. With each brushstroke, and each captured moment, you are not merely filling a blank space but unravelling the mysteries of your essence, your existence and your soul, presenting them to the world in their most authentic and unguarded form. There are indeed uncertainties and vulnerabilities and the thought of will the world receive your real self – as an artist.

The process of bringing your visions to life is immensely rewarding, yet it demands a dedication, patience, and a willingness to embark on a path of constant learning, experimentation, deep thinking and evolution.

Before we proceed let me share with you some basic steps to embark on this mesmerizing voyage as an artist:

- **Explore and Experiment:** Let your curiosity guide you through the vast and varied landscape of art. Dive into the exploration of different mediums and techniques—be it painting, digital art, photography, and so on. Allow yourself the freedom to experiment and discover what truly resonates with your spirit.

- **Educate Yourself:** The journey of learning in art go beyond the walls of formal education. Seek knowledge in the world around you—through online tutorials that bridge distances, workshops that build communities, and the quiet observation of life's unfolding drama. Be observant on how other artists showcase their work and how they promote their works. Each experience weaves a new thread into the rich tapestry of your artistic education.

- **Create Regularly:** Commit to the act of creation with dedication and prectice. Like the river that carves its path through the landscape, regular practice will sharpen your skills and define your artistic voice. Carve out moments from your days and nights to commune with your art, for it is in these moments of solitude and concentration that your true potential will reveal itself.

- **Build a Portfolio:** As your creations accumulate, so too should the curation of your portfolio. This collection, a reflection of your journey, passions, and evolution, speaks on your behalf to the world. It is through this portfolio that you will connect with galleries, clients, and fellow artists, sharing the essence of your journey.

- **Seek Feedback:** Open yourself to the reflections of the world. Share your art with friends, family, and the wider community to gain feedback. This exchange of perspectives is the crucible in which your growth as an artist is accelerated, offering invaluable insights and directions for improvement.

- **Establish an Online Presence:** In the digital age, your virtual presence is a lighthouse, guiding souls across the digital sea to your shores. Craft your digital galleries with care, ensuring each visitor's journey through your works brings them closer to the core of your artistic spirit.

- **Market Yourself**: Embrace the art of marketing with the same creative fervour that guides your hand. Understand the hearts and minds you wish to touch, and let your art serve as a bridge between your world and theirs.

- **Stay Inspired and Motivated:** Above all, remember to nurture the flame of inspiration. Seek it in the beauty of the world, in the annals of history, in the depths of emotion, and in the simplicity of the everyday. Let this inspiration fuel your creativity, pushing you to explore, create, and dream without limits.

Finding Your Art Style

Embarking on the journey to find your unique art style is akin to setting sail on a vast, uncharted ocean. It's a voyage of self-discovery, fraught with trials, revelations, and moments of sheer wonder. Your art style is more than just a signature; it's an extension of your innermost self, your perceptions, and how you interact with the world around you. Here are some ways you find your art style.

Embrace Exploration

The quest for your art style begins with a spirit of exploration. Immerse yourself in the diversity of the art world. Delve into the history of art, study the masters and the rebels, and absorb the vast spectrum of styles that have shaped the artistic landscape. Each piece you encounter is an example, illuminating paths you might choose to follow or diverge from. Remember, exploration is not confined to the visual arts alone; literature, music, and nature itself are fertile grounds for inspiration. Let your curiosity be boundless, for in the convergence of myriad influences, your unique style will begin to take root.

Experimentation Is Key

Your art style will not emerge fully formed but will evolve through continuous experimentation. This phase is your playground—an arena to test, combine, and alter techniques, mediums, and themes. It's where accidents can become breakthroughs, and where seemingly disparate elements can combine into something uniquely yours. Approach each piece with the mindset of a scientist conducting experiments, noting what resonates with you and what doesn't. Over time, patterns will emerge, preferences will solidify, and your style will start to crystallize.

Reflect and Refine

As you accumulate a body of work, take time to reflect on your creations. Lay them out, physically or digitally, and look for the common threads that weave through them. These threads—be they certain color palettes, subjects, or emotional tones—are the seeds of your style. Reflect on why these elements recur in your work. What do they reveal about your interests, your values, or the messages you wish to convey through your art? This introspection is crucial for understanding the essence of your style and refining it further.

Seek Feedback, But Stay True

Feedback from peers, mentors, and the art community can offer valuable perspectives on your evolving style. It can highlight strengths you might have overlooked and areas for improvement you hadn't considered. However, while external input can be enlightening, it's essential to remain true to your vision. Your art style should be a reflection of you, not a mirror of someone else's expectations or trends.

Patience and Persistence

Finding your art style is not a destination but a journey—one that is ongoing and ever-evolving. It could take a long time. Your style will change as you grow as an artist and as an individual. Embrace this evolution, knowing that each phase of your artistic journey contributes to the depth and richness of your style. Patience and persistence are your allies, reminding you that art, like life, is a process of continual growth and discovery.

Evolution of Artistic Styles of Iconic Artists

S/N	Artist	Approx. Duration to Find Style	Chronology of Styles
1	Pablo Picasso	1901-1909 (Blue and Rose Periods)	• Early Work (1890-1900) Realism/Post-Impressionism • Blue Period (1901-1904) • Rose Period (1905-1906) • African-influenced Period (1907-1909) • Cubism (1909 onwards)
2	Vincent van Gogh	1880-1888	• Early Work (1880-1885) Dark Colors, Dutch Peasant Genre • Paris Period (1886-1888) Impressionism, Lighter Palette • Final Period (1888-1890) Post-Impressionism, Vibrant Colors, Emotional Depth
3	Claude Monet	1860s-1872	• Early Work Realism • Impressionism (1872 onwards), with the painting "Impression, Sunrise" marking the beginning of his dedicated Impressionist style
4	Jackson Pollock	1938-1947	• Early Work Regionalism • Surrealism and Abstract (early 1940s) • Drip Painting (1947 onwards)
5	Georgia O'Keeffe	1910-1920s	• Early Work Charcoal Abstractions • Synthetic Cubism • American Modernism/Precisionism and large-scale flowers
6	Wassily Kandinsky	1896-1911	• Early Work Realism/Impressionism • Expressionism (1908-1911) • Abstract Art (1911 onwards)

7	Frida Kahlo	1925-1930s	<ul><li>Early Work Folk Art and Portraiture</li><li>Surrealism/Personal Style (1930s onwards), though she rejected the "Surrealist" label</li></ul>
8	Salvador Dalí	1920s-1929	<ul><li>Early Work Impressionism, Cubism</li><li>Surrealism (1929 onwards) after joining the Surrealists</li></ul>
9	Henri Matisse	1890-1905	<ul><li>Early Work Traditional</li><li>Fauvism (1905 onwards), with "Woman with a Hat" marking his Fauvist debut</li></ul>
10	Michelangelo	Early works (1488-1492) to Sistine Chapel (1508-1512)	<ul><li>Early Work Sculpture in the round, Pietà</li><li>High Renaissance style fully realized in the Sistine Chapel ceiling</li></ul>
11	Leonardo da Vinci	1470s-1480s	<ul><li>Early Work Verrocchio's Workshop, Early Renaissance</li><li>High Renaissance style, culminating in works like "The Last Supper" and "Mona Lisa"</li></ul>
12	Rembrandt	1625-1630s	<ul><li>Early Work Baroque, Caravaggisti Influence</li><li>Mature Style characterized by dramatic use of light and shadow, emotional depth (1630s onwards)</li></ul>
13	Mark Rothko	1920s-1940s	<ul><li>Early Work Realism</li><li>Surrealism</li><li>Abstract Expressionism (late 1940s onwards), with his signature Color Field paintings</li></ul>
14	Andy Warhol	1950s-1962	<ul><li>Early Work Commercial Illustration</li><li>Pop Art (1962 onwards) with "Campbell's Soup Cans" and "Marilyn Diptych"</li></ul>

15	Yayoi Kusama	1950s-1960s	• Early Work Nihonga style • Abstract Expressionism in New York • Pop Art and Minimalism, with her signature polka dots emerging prominently in the 1960s

Evolving Perspectives on Artists and Their Work

Art is not static; it's a dynamic reflection of the ever-changing currents of society, culture, and human consciousness. Artists, like seers of their time, capture the essence of their era, often pushing boundaries and challenging norms. Yet, the reception of their work can be a complex interplay of factors, influenced by shifting artistic values, historical contexts, market dynamics, and cultural shifts. Unfortunately, the artistic styles of many artists are often truly appreciated only after they have passed away, leading to widespread recognition. This might be due to the following:

1. Changing Artistic Values and Trends

Artistic values and trends are in constant flux, and what may not have been appreciated during an artist's lifetime might gain significance as cultural and aesthetic sensibilities evolve. Historical context is crucial; societal changes can transform the way art is interpreted and valued. An artist's work may be ahead of its time, with future generations finding new relevance and meaning in it that contemporaries did not.

2. Rediscovery and Reevaluation

In some cases, an artist's work is rediscovered long after their death, leading to a reevaluation of their contribution to the art world. This can be triggered by academic research, exhibitions, or a renewed interest in certain art movements. As art historians dig deeper into periods and styles, they might uncover overlooked artists whose work gains new appreciation.

3. Romanticization of the Artist's Life

There's a cultural fascination with the archetype of the "tortured artist" who gains fame after death. This romanticized view can lead to increased interest in an artist's work once their life story, often marked by struggle, becomes widely known. The personal narratives of artists like Vincent van Gogh or Modigliani have contributed to the mystique and allure of their art.

4. Market Dynamics

The art market plays a significant role in the recognition of artists. Posthumously, the supply of an artist's work becomes finite, potentially increasing its value. Auctions and sales can draw attention to previously undervalued artists, leading to a reassessment of their importance and influence within the art world.

5. Cultural and Technological Shifts

Changes in technology and culture can also affect the appreciation of an artist's work. For instance, the advent of color photography brought new recognition to early photographers once their contributions could be fully appreciated. Similarly, social and political shifts can lead to a reevaluation of artists who tackled themes that become more relevant or understood over time.

6. Institutional Recognition

Museums, galleries, and academic institutions play a crucial role in the canonization of artists. Curatorial decisions, exhibitions, and scholarly work can spotlight artists who were overlooked or marginalized during their lifetimes. This institutional recognition can catalyze a broader appreciation of their styles and contributions.

Identifying Your Unique Selling Proposition

The journey to successfully market and sell your art begins with a solid foundation. This foundation consists of three crucial elements:

- Identifying your unique selling proposition (USP),
- Setting clear goals and expectations, and
- Understanding your audience. Each element plays a vital role in shaping your approach to the art market and defines the trajectory of your art career.

Identifying Your Unique Selling Proposition

Your unique selling proposition (USP) is what sets your art apart from the countless other pieces available in the market. It's the reason people choose your work over others. Identifying your USP involves introspection and a keen understanding of your art and its place in the broader market.

Identifying your Unique Selling Proposition (USP) delves deeper into understanding not just what your art looks like, but what it represents and the emotions it evokes. It requires you to analyze not only your technical skills but also the conceptual aspects of your work. Consider questions such as: What themes or messages recur in your art? What emotions do you aim to convey? How do you approach your subjects or materials differently from others? Moreover, studying the market and recognizing gaps or niches where your art can uniquely fill a need can also inform your USP. Essentially, your USP is the essence of your artistic identity distilled into a compelling reason for others to connect with and choose your art.

Reflect on Your Art: Begin by considering what drives you to create. Is it your technique, the themes you explore, or the stories behind each piece? Perhaps it's the materials you use or the way you play with colors. Your motivation and approach to creating art can be a significant part of your USP.

Analyze Your Audience's Reaction: Pay attention to which aspects of your work resonate most with your audience. Is there a particular piece or style that receives more attention or praise? Feedback from your audience can offer valuable insights into what makes your art unique.

Evaluate the Market: Look at other artists who create similar work. What can you offer that they don't? This could be something tangible, like a unique method or material, or intangible, such as evoking a particular feeling or memory.

Articulate Your USP: Once you've identified what makes your art unique, learn to articulate it clearly. This will not only help in marketing your art but will also guide you in staying true to your vision.

Setting Goals and Expectations

Setting clear, achievable goals and having realistic expectations are crucial for measuring success and maintaining motivation.

Short-term and Long-term Goals:

Define what success looks like to you in the short term (next few months to a year) and the long term (next few years). These goals could range from selling a certain number of pieces to securing a gallery exhibition or building a robust online following.

S.M.A.R.T Goals:

Ensure your goals are Specific, Measurable, Achievable, Relevant, and Time-bound. For example, instead of "sell more art," aim for "sell 10 pieces in the next three months through online channels."

Set Realistic Expectations:

Understand that growth in the art world can be slow and unpredictable. Setting realistic expectations helps in managing frustrations and staying focused on long-term success.

Understanding Your Audience

Knowing who your art appeals to is crucial for effective marketing and sales strategies.

Define Your Ideal Buyer:

Create a profile of your ideal buyer. Consider factors like age, income level, interests, and where they likely spend their time online and offline. This information will guide where and how you market your art.

Engage with Your Audience:

Utilize social media, art shows, and exhibitions to interact with your audience. Listen to their feedback and observe which pieces draw more interest.

Research Your Audience's Buying Behaviour:

Understanding how, when, and why your audience buys art will help you tailor your sales approach. Do they buy art for investment, decoration, or emotional connection?

Adapt and Evolve:

As you gain more insights into your audience, be prepared to refine your understanding and adjust your marketing strategies accordingly. The art market is dynamic, and flexibility can be a significant asset.

Chapter 2

Pricing Your Art

Navigating the intricate process of pricing artwork is often a daunting task for emerging artists stepping into the market. It entails a delicate balance between recognizing the value of your creativity, time, and expertise while also aligning with the market's perceptions and willingness to invest. Chapter 2 of this guide is dedicated to unraveling the complexities of pricing your art, offering invaluable insights into the factors to weigh, strategies to employ, and how to adapt your pricing over time.

Delving into the difficulties of pricing art requires a multifaceted approach. Artists must factor in various elements, including the cost of materials, the labour invested in each piece, market demand, artistic experience, and recognition, as well as the size and complexity of their creations. Understanding these factors provides a foundation of how to assign value to your work effectively.

Moreover, this chapter illuminates diverse pricing strategies artists can employ, from the straightforward cost-plus pricing method to the more value-based and tiered pricing approaches. Each strategy comes with its own set of considerations and implications, offering artists the flexibility to tailor their pricing approach to their unique circumstances and target audience.

Furthermore, as the art market evolves and artists progress in their careers, it becomes imperative to revisit and refine pricing strategies over time.

Artists should recognize that pricing art is one of the most challenging aspects for entering the art market. It's a delicate balance between valuing your time, skill, and the market's willingness to pay. Here are factors to consider:

Factors to Consider When Pricing Art

Cost of Materials: Start with the basics by calculating the cost of materials used in each piece. This includes everything from canvas and paint to framing and any other materials that contribute to the creation of your work. There are also hidden costs such as local transportation, and storage.

Time and Labor: Consider the amount of time you spend creating each piece. Assigning a value to your time can be challenging but think about what hourly rate would make the work sustainable for you. Remember, your time includes not just the act of creation but also the research, planning, and any post-creation finishing touches. There are no clear ways to value your time, for example you may be new in art but in other fields, you must have reached a peak so you can not use the rates in the field you have been working in to calculate your rather assume a rate for average artists in your area.

Market Demand: The demand for your art plays a significant role in pricing. If you have more buyers than pieces available, you might consider increasing your prices. Conversely, if you're struggling to make sales, you may need to adjust your pricing strategy.

Artistic Experience and Recognition: Generally, as your career progresses, your prices can increase. This is tied not just to your skill level but also to your recognition in the art world. Have you received awards? Have you been featured in galleries or publications? These accolades can justify higher prices.

Size and Complexity: Larger and more complex pieces typically command higher prices due to the increased materials and time required. Generally, the size of the art might be directly proportional to its costs, but then also experience counts a great deal.

Comparable Sales: Look at the prices of art similar to yours in style, medium, and artist experience. This research can help you gauge where your prices should fall within the market.

Strategies for Pricing Your Work

Cost-Plus Pricing:

Add up your costs (materials and time) and add a markup to ensure a profit. This method is straightforward but may not always align with market value.

Price=Cost of Materials + Labor Cost + Overhead + Profit Margin

Where:

Cost of Materials:
The total cost of all materials used in creating the art piece.

Labor Cost:
The value of the artist's time and effort spent on creating the art piece. This can be calculated by multiplying the number of hours spent on the piece by an hourly rate that reflects the artist's skill level and desired income.

Overhead:
Any additional costs incurred in the production process, such as studio rent, utilities, or equipment depreciation. This can be calculated as a percentage of the total cost of materials and labor.

Profit Margin:
The desired profit margin for the artist, typically expressed as a percentage of the total cost of materials, labor, and overhead.

Value-Based Pricing:

Price based on the perceived value of your work to the buyer. This can be more subjective but allows for higher pricing for pieces that evoke strong emotional responses or have a particular significance.

Price=Perceived Value to Buyer

This formula relies on the perceived value of the artwork to the buyer, rather than the costs incurred by the artist. It takes into account factors such as the emotional impact of the artwork, its cultural significance, or its relevance to the buyer's interests.

Tiered Pricing:

Offer different tiers of artwork at varying prices. This could include original works, limited edition prints, and open edition prints. Tiered pricing can make your art accessible to a broader audience while still valuing your most exclusive pieces appropriately.

Price=Base Price + Additional Price for Premium Tiers

In tiered pricing, the artist offers different tiers of artwork at varying prices. This formula involves setting a base price for the artwork and adding additional prices for premium tiers, such as limited edition prints or exclusive commissions.

Psychological Pricing:

Setting prices just below a round number (e.g., $499 instead of $500) can make prices seem lower than they are, potentially making your art more attractive to buyers.

Price=Round Number−Small Adjustment

Psychological pricing involves setting prices just below a round number to make them seem lower than they are. This formula subtracts a small adjustment from a round number to create a price that is psychologically more attractive to buyers.

Adjusting Prices Over Time

Adapting to the evolving dynamics of the art market, particularly in terms of pricing, is crucial for artists seeking sustainability and growth in their careers. Here we delve into the essential practice of adjusting prices over time, recognizing the fluid nature of artistic value and market demand. Regular reviews of pricing strategies serve as a cornerstone, offering artists the opportunity to recalibrate their pricing structures in response to various factors such as acquired skills, increased recognition, or fluctuations in the cost of materials. Moreover, we emphasize the importance of gradual price increases, avoiding sudden spikes that may alienate existing collectors while ensuring that the artist's work remains accessible to new audiences. Effective communication of price changes is also paramount, fostering transparency with collectors and creating a sense of urgency among potential buyers. Additionally, the chapter explores strategies for accommodating special circumstances, such as offering discounts to loyal collectors, while maintaining the consistency and integrity of the artwork's value. Through these insights and guidelines, artists can navigate the complexities of price adjustments with confidence, ultimately fostering long-term relationships with collectors and sustaining a thriving artistic practice. Here are some thoughts:

- **Regular Reviews:** Schedule regular reviews of your pricing strategy. This could be annually or bi-annually. Adjust your prices based on new skills acquired, recognition, and changes in the cost of materials.

- **Gradual Increases:** When increasing prices, do so gradually. Sudden, significant hikes can alienate existing collectors. A rule of thumb is to increase prices by 10-15% at a time.

- **Communicate Changes:** If you have a following, communicate any price changes ahead of time. This can create urgency among potential buyers and shows transparency to your existing collectors.

- **Special Circumstances:** Consider offering discounts or special pricing for loyal collectors, but do this sparingly. Your art's value should be consistent, and frequent discounts can undermine this.

Chapter 3

Finding Your Art Collectors and Buyers

In the vast landscape of the art market, connecting with the right collectors and buyers is essential for artists to thrive. This chapter explores various strategies and avenues for identifying and engaging with potential collectors, ultimately expanding your audience and enhancing your artistic career.

- **Art Galleries and Exhibitions:** One of the traditional avenues for finding collectors is through art galleries and exhibitions. Participating in group shows or securing solo exhibitions can expose your work to a wider audience, including art enthusiasts, collectors, and gallery owners who may be interested in acquiring your art.

- **Online Platforms:** The digital age has revolutionized the way artists connect with buyers. Utilize online platforms such as social media, artist websites, and online marketplaces to showcase your art to a global audience. Platforms like Instagram, Facebook, and Pinterest allow you to share your work directly with potential collectors and engage with them on a personal level.

- **Art Fairs and Markets:** Art fairs and markets provide opportunities for artists to interact with collectors face-to-face and showcase their work in a dynamic and engaging environment. Research local and international art fairs that align with your artistic style and target audience, and consider participating as an exhibitor or visitor to network with collectors and buyers.

- **Networking Events:** Building relationships with fellow artists, collectors, and industry professionals can be invaluable in expanding your collector base. Attend art openings, networking events, and artist talks to connect with like-minded individuals and establish meaningful connections that may lead to future sales or collaborations.

- **Art Consultants and Advisors:** Collaborating with art consultants and advisors can help you tap into their networks of collectors and buyers. These professionals provide expertise and guidance in navigating the art market, connecting artists with potential buyers, and facilitating sales transactions.

- **Commissioned Work:** Offering commissioned work is another avenue for finding buyers who have a specific vision or aesthetic in mind. Promote your commission services through your website, social media, and word-of-mouth referrals to attract clients who are interested in personalized artwork tailored to their preferences.

- **Local Community Engagement:** Engaging with your local community through art workshops, public art projects, or community events can raise your profile as an artist and attract local collectors who value supporting artists within their community.

- **Art Collectors' Organizations and Clubs:** Joining art collectors' organizations or clubs can provide access to a network of established collectors who are passionate about supporting emerging artists. Participate in club events, exhibitions, and auctions to showcase your work and forge connections with potential buyers.

Chapter 4

Presenting Your Art

Presenting your art effectively is crucial in capturing the attention of potential buyers and galleries. This chapter focuses on creating a strong portfolio, offering professional photography tips for your art, and writing compelling descriptions. These elements combined will ensure your art is seen in the best light and engages your audience.

Creating a Strong Portfolio

- **Curate Your Best Work:** Your portfolio should be a collection of your best work, not necessarily all of your work. Choose pieces that represent your style, skill, and the themes you explore. Aim for diversity in your selection to show your range, but keep it cohesive enough to demonstrate a clear, personal voice.

- **Organize Thoughtfully:** How you organize your portfolio can impact how your work is perceived. Consider grouping pieces by theme, medium, or chronology, depending on what best showcases your development and range as an artist.

- **Include Professional Documentation:** For each piece, include title, medium, dimensions, and year created. If relevant, also include a brief statement about the work. This information is crucial for galleries and collectors and helps in building a professional image.

- **Digital Presence:** In today's art market, a digital portfolio is indispensable. Use platforms that cater to artists and creatives to display your work, such as personal websites or art-specific networks. Ensure your digital portfolio is easy to navigate and visually appealing.

- **Professional Photography Tips for Your Art**

- **Natural Lighting:** Photograph your work in natural, indirect light to avoid harsh shadows and reflections. Overcast days are ideal for even lighting.

- **Steady Camera:** Use a tripod to ensure your camera is steady. A remote shutter release or your camera's timer function can help avoid any shake when taking the photo.

- **Correct Angle:** Photograph your artwork head-on, ensuring your camera is centered and parallel to the art to avoid distortion. For three-dimensional works, consider multiple angles to fully capture the piece.

- **High Resolution**: Use the highest resolution setting on your camera to ensure that your images are clear and detailed, suitable for both online viewing and print.

- **Editing:** Minimal post-processing can be done to adjust the lighting and color to match the original piece as closely as possible. Avoid over-editing, as this can misrepresent your work.

Writing Compelling Descriptions

- **Tell a Story:** Each piece of art has a story. Share yours. Whether it's the inspiration behind the work, the process of creating it, or the meaning it holds, telling this story can create a connection with your audience.

- **Be Descriptive:** Use descriptive language to convey the colors, textures, and emotions of your piece. This can be especially important for online sales, where buyers can't see the work in person.

- **Keep it Accessible:** While it's important to be descriptive, also ensure your language is accessible. Avoid jargon that might alienate those not familiar with art terminology.

- **Include a Call to Action:** If you're selling your art directly, include a call to action in your description. Invite viewers to imagine the piece in their space, or suggest they contact you for more details.

Documentation of Art for Gallery Representation

Professional documentation of art is essential for artists seeking to exhibit their work in galleries. This documentation serves multiple purposes, including providing a comprehensive record of the artwork, facilitating marketing and promotional efforts, and ensuring proper handling and care of the pieces. Here's a detailed explanation of the key components of professional documentation suitable for a gallery:

- **High-Quality Images:** High-resolution photographs of the artwork are crucial for showcasing its details, colors, and textures accurately. These images serve as the primary visual representation of the artwork for promotional materials, online galleries, and exhibition catalogs. Photographs should be well-lit, properly focused, and captured from various angles to provide a comprehensive view of the piece.

- **Artist Statement:** An artist statement provides insight into the artist's inspiration, creative process, and artistic vision. It offers viewers a deeper understanding of the artwork and its significance, enhancing their appreciation and engagement. The artist statement should be concise, articulate, and reflective of the artist's unique perspective and style.

- **Artwork Description:** Each piece of art should be accompanied by a detailed description that includes information such as title, medium, dimensions, and date of creation. Additional details, such as the inspiration behind the artwork or notable techniques used, can provide further context and enrich the viewer's experience.

- **Certificate of Authenticity:** A certificate of authenticity verifies the authenticity and provenance of the artwork, providing assurance to collectors and buyers. It typically includes information such as the artist's name, artwork title, medium, dimensions, date of creation, and signature. A unique serial number or holographic seal may also be included to prevent forgery.

- **Exhibition History:** A record of the artwork's exhibition history demonstrates its pedigree and establishes the artist's credibility within the art world. This information should include details of previous exhibitions, including the name of the gallery or venue, exhibition dates, and any awards or honors received.

- **Condition Report:** A condition report documents the current condition of the artwork, noting any visible damage, imperfections, or alterations. This information is crucial for galleries and collectors to assess the artwork's condition accurately and ensure proper handling and care during transportation and display.

- **Documentation of Conservation and Restoration:** If applicable, documentation of any conservation or restoration work performed on the artwork should be included. This information provides transparency regarding the artwork's treatment history and ensures that conservation standards have been adhered to.

- **Inventory Management:** Maintaining a detailed inventory of artworks, including photographs, descriptions, and relevant documentation, is essential for organizational purposes and tracking the whereabouts of each piece. Digital inventory management systems can streamline this process and facilitate efficient cataloguing and retrieval of information.

Packaging Your Art and Handling It For Sales

Packaging your art and handling it for sales is a critical aspect of ensuring that your artwork arrives safely to its destination and makes a positive impression on potential buyers. Here's a guide on how to package your art and handle it for sales:

- **Selecting Appropriate Packaging Materials:** Choose packaging materials that provide adequate protection for your artwork during transit. This typically includes sturdy cardboard boxes, bubble wrap, packing peanuts, foam boards, and tape. Consider the size, weight, and fragility of your artwork when selecting packaging materials.

- **Protecting the Artwork:** Wrap the artwork securely in acid-free tissue paper or glassine to protect it from scratches, dust, and moisture. For framed pieces, use corner protectors to prevent damage to the frame during transit. If shipping multiple pieces together, separate them with cardboard or foam board to prevent them from rubbing against each other.

- **Securing the Artwork in the Packaging:** Place the wrapped artwork in a snug-fitting box lined with bubble wrap or packing peanuts to provide cushioning. Ensure that the artwork is centered and secured within the box to prevent it from shifting during transit. Use additional padding or filler material as needed to fill any empty spaces and minimize movement.

- **Labelling and Marking the Packaging:** Clearly label the packaging with the recipient's name, address, and contact information, as well as your own return address. Include "Fragile" or "Handle with Care" labels to alert handlers to the delicate nature of the contents. For international shipments, include customs forms and any required documentation.

- **Choosing a Reliable Shipping Method:** Select a shipping method that offers tracking, insurance, and delivery confirmation to ensure the safe and timely arrival of your artwork. Consider factors such as transit time, cost, and destination when choosing a shipping carrier or courier service. Communicate with the buyer to coordinate shipping logistics and provide them with tracking information once the artwork has been dispatched.

- **Handling In-Person Sales:** When selling artwork in person, handle it with care and professionalism to create a positive impression on potential buyers. Use white gloves when handling delicate or sensitive artwork to prevent fingerprints and damage. Provide buyers with an opportunity to inspect the artwork closely and ask any questions they may have about the piece.

- **Offering Packaging Options for Buyers:** If selling artwork in person, offer packaging options for buyers to safely transport their purchases home. Provide protective sleeves or portfolios for unframed works on paper, and offer to wrap framed pieces in bubble wrap or tissue paper for added protection. Ensure that the packaging is sturdy and secure to prevent damage during transport.

List of Commonly Used Materials for Handling Art

- **Cardboard Boxes:** Sturdy cardboard boxes in various sizes to accommodate different artwork dimensions.

- **Bubble Wrap:** Cushioning material to wrap around the artwork for protection against impact and vibration during transit.

- **Packing Peanuts:** Loose-fill packing material to fill empty spaces within boxes and provide additional cushioning.

- **Foam Boards:** Rigid foam boards to protect framed artwork and provide support during transit.

- **Acid-Free Tissue Paper:** Thin, non-reactive tissue paper to wrap artwork and protect it from scratches, dust, and moisture.

- **Glassine:** Smooth, translucent paper used as an additional layer of protection for delicate artwork, especially works on paper.

- **Corner Protectors:** Protective covers for the corners of framed artwork to prevent damage to the frame during transit.

- **Tape:** Strong packing tape to seal boxes securely and reinforce seams.

- **Labels and Markers:** Labels for addressing packages and marking boxes with handling instructions such as "Fragile" or "Handle with Care."

- **Shipping Labels:** Pre-printed labels with recipient and sender information for affixing to packages.

- **Customs Forms:** Required documentation for international shipments, including customs declaration forms and invoices.

- **White Gloves:** Cotton gloves worn when handling delicate or sensitive artwork to prevent fingerprints and damage.

- **Packaging Tape Dispenser:** Tool for dispensing packing tape quickly and efficiently during packaging.

- **Scissors or Box Cutter:** Cutting tools for trimming materials and opening boxes.

- **Packaging Fillers:** Additional padding materials such as foam inserts, air pillows, or crumpled paper for extra protection.

- **Rigid Mailers:** Sturdy envelopes or mailers for shipping flat artwork or small prints.

- **Shipping Labels and Stickers:** Labels for indicating special handling instructions or shipping preferences, such as "Do Not Bend" or "Priority Mail."

- **Stretch Wrap:** Clear plastic wrap used to secure multiple pieces together or protect artwork from moisture during transit.

Art Canvas and How to Make it

(a) Art Canvas Standard Sizes

Art canvas comes in a variety of standard sizes to accommodate different artistic needs and preferences. Common sizes for stretched canvases include:

- **Small Sizes:** These are typically around 8"x10" or 9"x12", suitable for small-scale paintings or studies.

- **Medium Sizes:** Medium-sized canvases range from 12"x16" to 18"x24", offering a versatile canvas size for various artistic projects.

- **Large Sizes:** Larger canvases, such as 24"x36" or 30"x40", provide ample space for more ambitious and detailed artworks.

- **Custom Sizes:** Artists may also choose to work on custom-sized canvases tailored to their specific requirements or creative vision.

Importance of Stretching Your Canvas

Stretching canvas is a crucial step in preparing it for painting. Stretching not only provides a smooth and taut surface for painting but also ensures the longevity and stability of the artwork over time. By stretching canvas properly, artists can minimize the risk of sagging, warping, or wrinkling, resulting in a professional and durable painting surface.

How to Stretch Your Canvas

Stretching canvas requires careful attention to detail and a few essential tools. Here's a step-by-step guide on how to stretch your canvas:

Materials Needed:

- Canvas
- Wooden stretcher bars
- Canvas pliers
- Staple gun or hammer and staples
- Scissors
- Canvas stretching wedges (optional)

Prepare the Stretcher Bars:

- Assemble the wooden stretcher bars to create a frame that matches the desired size of your canvas.
- Ensure that the corners are square and the bars fit together snugly.

Position the Canvas:

Lay the canvas flat on a clean, flat surface with the front side facing down. Center the stretcher frame over the canvas, leaving excess canvas around the edges for stretching.

Start Stretching:

- Begin by folding one edge of the canvas over the top stretcher bar and staple it in the center.
- Move to the opposite side and pull the canvas taut, then staple it in the center.
- Continue stapling along the edges, alternating sides and working outward from the center to maintain tension evenly.

Stretch the Corners:

- Fold the corners of the canvas neatly over the stretcher bars, creating crisp, diagonal folds.
- Staple the folded corners securely to the stretcher bars, ensuring that the canvas remains taut.

Trim Excess Canvas:

- Use scissors to trim any excess canvas from the edges, leaving a clean and tidy finish.

Optional: Apply Canvas Stretching Wedges:

If desired, insert canvas stretching wedges into the corners of the stretcher frame and tap them gently with a hammer to further tighten the canvas.
Inspect and Adjust:

Once the canvas is stretched, inspect it for any loose areas or wrinkles.
Make any necessary adjustments to ensure that the canvas is evenly stretched and free of imperfections.

Navigating Finances in the Art Market: Taxes, Shipping, and Other Cost Considerations

Dealing with taxes, shipping, and other costs is an essential aspect of selling art professionally. Here's a comprehensive guide on how to navigate these financial considerations:

- **Understanding Taxes:** Artists who sell their work are typically subject to various taxes, including income tax and sales tax. It's essential to understand your tax obligations based on your location and the specific regulations governing art sales in your region. Consult with a tax professional or accountant to ensure compliance with tax laws and maximize deductions for business expenses.

- **Sales Tax:** In many jurisdictions, artists are required to collect and remit sales tax on art sales. Research the sales tax rates applicable to art sales in your area and determine whether you need to register for a sales tax permit. Keep accurate records of sales transactions, including the amount of sales tax collected, to facilitate tax reporting and compliance.

- **Income Tax:** Artists are also responsible for reporting art sales as income on their tax returns. Keep detailed records of all art sales, including sales receipts, invoices, and payment records. Deduct any legitimate business expenses, such as art supplies, studio rent, marketing costs, and shipping expenses, to reduce taxable income.

- **Shipping Costs:** When selling art, consider the cost of shipping and handling, which can vary depending on the size, weight, and destination of the artwork. Factor shipping costs into your pricing strategy to ensure that you cover expenses while remaining competitive in the market. Offer shipping options to buyers, such as standard shipping, expedited shipping, or local pickup, and clearly communicate shipping policies and fees upfront.

- **Packaging Materials:** Invest in quality packaging materials to ensure that your artwork arrives safely to its destination. Consider the cost of packaging materials, such as boxes, bubble wrap, packing peanuts, and tape, when calculating shipping expenses. Factor these costs into your pricing strategy to cover packaging expenses and provide a seamless buying experience for customers.

- **Insurance:** Consider purchasing shipping insurance to protect valuable artworks against loss or damage during transit. Insurance premiums are typically based on the declared value of the artwork and the chosen coverage limits. Evaluate the cost-benefit of insurance coverage and communicate insurance options to buyers to offer peace of mind and mitigate risk.

- **Handling Fees:** Some artists may charge handling fees to cover the time and labor involved in preparing artwork for shipment. Determine a reasonable handling fee based on the complexity of packaging and the level of service provided. Clearly communicate handling fees to buyers to avoid misunderstandings and ensure transparency in pricing.

- **International Sales:** When selling art internationally, be aware of additional costs and considerations, such as customs duties, import taxes, and international shipping fees. Research international shipping regulations and customs requirements for artwork to avoid delays or unexpected expenses. Clearly communicate international shipping policies and fees to buyers to facilitate smooth transactions and minimize disputes.

Chapter 5

Online Marketing Strategies

Marketing for art is a multifaceted endeavor that goes beyond simply showcasing artwork; it's about connecting with audiences, cultivating relationships, and creating opportunities for engagement and appreciation. In today's digital age, artists have unprecedented access to global audiences through online platforms and social media channels, revolutionizing the way art is promoted and consumed. From establishing a compelling online presence to networking with industry professionals and participating in exhibitions, marketing for art comprise a diverse range of strategies aimed at elevating artists' visibility, attracting collectors and buyers, and fostering long-term connections with art enthusiasts. In this dynamic landscape, artists must navigate the complexities of marketing to effectively promote their artwork and navigate the competitive art market.

Online marketing is crucial for artists looking to sell their work and build their reputation. There are various effective strategies such as building an artist website, leveraging social media, utilizing email marketing, and understanding the basics of SEO. These tools can help you reach a wider audience, engage with potential buyers, and grow your art business.

Building an Artist Website

- **Showcase Your Portfolio:** Your website should highlight your art. Include high-quality images, detailed descriptions, and the stories behind your work. Make sure it's easy for visitors to navigate through your portfolio.

- **About Page:** Include an about page with your biography, artist statement, and a professional photo. This helps build a connection with your audience by sharing your journey and the inspiration behind your work.

- **Contact Information:** Make it easy for visitors to contact you. Include a contact form or your email address, social media links, and possibly your phone number.

- **Sales and Commissions:** If you're selling your art directly from your website, include a shop section with clear pricing, shipping information, and terms of sale. For commissions, outline the process, pricing, and how clients can get in touch with you for custom work.

- **Mobile Optimization:** Ensure your website is mobile-friendly. With an increasing number of users accessing the web through mobile devices, your site must look good and function well on smartphones and tablets.

Leveraging Social Media to Your Advantage

- **Choose the Right Platforms:** Focus on platforms where your target audience is most active. Instagram and Pinterest are particularly visual, making them ideal for artists.

- **Consistency is Key:** Post regularly to keep your audience engaged. Share not just your final pieces but also your process, behind-the-scenes looks, and even your daily life as an artist to build a more personal connection.

- **Engage with Your Audience:** Respond to comments, messages, and engage with other artists and potential buyers. Building relationships can turn followers into fans and customers.

- **Use Hashtags and Tags Wisely:** Research relevant hashtags to reach a wider audience. Tagging art galleries, art collectors, and using specific art-related hashtags can increase your visibility.

- **Promote Your Website:** Use your social media profiles to drive traffic to your artist website where followers can view your full portfolio and purchase your work.

Email Marketing for Artists

- **Build Your List:** Start collecting email addresses from your website, social media channels, and art shows. Offer something of value, like a free art print or an ebook about your art, in exchange for signing up.

- **Regular Newsletters:** Send out regular newsletters with updates on your latest work, upcoming shows, and behind-the-scenes content. Keep your audience informed and engaged with your art journey.

- **Exclusive Offers:** Provide exclusive offers to your email subscribers, such as early access to new pieces, discounts, or limited edition prints. This can encourage sales and make your subscribers feel valued.

- **Personalization:** Personalize your emails where possible. Use your subscribers' names and segment your list to send more targeted, relevant content.

SEO Basics for Artists

- **Keywords:** Identify keywords that potential buyers might use to find art like yours. Include these keywords naturally in your website's content, titles, and meta descriptions.

- **Image Optimization:** Use descriptive file names and alt text for your images. This not only helps visually impaired users understand what the image depicts but also improves your site's SEO.

- **Mobile Optimization:** A mobile-friendly website is crucial for SEO. Google prioritizes mobile-optimized sites in its search results.

- **Content:** Regularly update your website with fresh content. Blogging about your art, creative process, and industry insights can help improve your site's ranking.

- **Backlinks:** Get other reputable websites to link back to your site. This could be through collaborations, guest blogging, or getting featured in online galleries and art publications.

Chapter 6
Offline Marketing Strategies

While online marketing has become a cornerstone of promoting art in the digital age, traditional offline methods remain powerful tools for artists to sell their work and build their reputation. Here we explore effective offline marketing strategies, including networking in the art world, participating in art shows and galleries, and collaborating with local businesses.

Networking in the Art World

- **Attend Art Events:** Regularly attend art fairs, openings, workshops, and talks. These events provide opportunities to meet other artists, gallery owners, and art enthusiasts who can offer support, advice, and opportunities.

- **Join Art Organizations:** Become a member of local or national art organizations. These groups often host events, exhibitions, and provide resources for artists looking to grow their network.

- **Volunteer:** Offering your time and skills to art events or organizations can be a great way to make connections while contributing to the art community.

- **Create Business Cards:** Have professional business cards ready to hand out when you meet someone new. Include your name, contact information, and website or social media handles.

- **Follow Up:** After meeting someone new, follow up with an email or a message on social media. A simple message expressing your appreciation for the conversation and interest in keeping in touch can go a long way.

Participating in Art Shows and Galleries

Navigating the world of art exhibitions and shows requires a strategic approach that goes beyond mere participation; it involves a deliberate search for opportunities that align with your artistic vision and resonate with your target audience. Researching art shows and gallery exhibitions allows artists to strategically select events where their work will have the greatest impact, increasing the chances of connecting with potential collectors and buyers. Moreover, preparation is key, and having a professional portfolio ready to showcase your best work, along with tailored pitches for each venue, demonstrates professionalism and enthusiasm. In this competitive landscape, artists must also consider the storytelling aspect of their artwork, seeking pieces that evoke emotions and personal resonance to captivate viewers and enhance their connection with potential collectors. Additionally, attention to detail in the presentation of artwork, coupled with active engagement with attendees during shows, fosters deeper understanding and appreciation, ultimately leading to meaningful relationships and potential sales opportunities. Effective follow-up after events ensures that connections made are nurtured and maintained, paving the way for continued engagement and future collaborations. Here are the key steps:

- **Research Opportunities:** Look for art shows and gallery exhibitions that align with your style and target audience. This includes local art fairs, group shows, and juried exhibitions. Researching opportunities allows you to select events where your work will resonate most with attendees, increasing the likelihood of connecting with potential collectors and buyers.

- **Prepare Your Portfolio:** Have a professional portfolio ready to show gallery owners and exhibition curators. Include your best work, artist statement, and any press materials or accolades. Your portfolio serves as your visual resume, showcasing the breadth and depth of your artistic talent while providing insight into your artistic vision and accomplishments.

- **Pitch Your Work:** Don't be afraid to reach out to galleries or show organizers with a proposal. Tailor each pitch to the venue, explaining why your work is a good fit for their space or event. Highlighting the unique qualities of your art and its relevance to the venue's audience demonstrates your professionalism and enthusiasm, increasing the likelihood of securing exhibition opportunities.

- **Look for Compelling Stories:** When selecting artwork to present at art shows and galleries, look for pieces that tell compelling stories or evoke strong emotions. Art with a narrative or personal resonance can captivate viewers and create a deeper connection, making it more likely to resonate with potential collectors and buyers.

- **Value Presentation:** Pay attention to how your artwork is presented at art shows and galleries. Consider factors such as framing, lighting, and arrangement to enhance the visual impact and appeal of your pieces. Thoughtful presentation not only showcases your artwork in the best possible light but also reinforces its value and significance to viewers.

- **Engage Attendees:** When participating in shows, be present and engage with attendees. Discuss your work, answer questions, and collect contact information for follow-up. Building personal connections with attendees allows you to share the inspiration and meaning behind your artwork, fostering a deeper understanding and appreciation among potential collectors and buyers. Additionally, collecting contact information enables you to follow up with interested individuals, further nurturing relationships and potential sales opportunities.

- **Follow Up:** After the event, reach out to contacts you made, thank them for their interest, and keep them informed about your upcoming work and events.

International Art Shows

S/N	Art Show	Location	Estimated Period	Estimated Attendance Number	Brief Information	Website URL
1	Venice Biennial	Venice, Italy	Every two years (June-November)	>300,000	One of the oldest and most prestigious contemporary art exhibitions, featuring international artists.	labiennale.org
2	Art Basel	Basel, Switzerland & Miami, USA	Annually (June 14-17 in Basel)	N/A	Premier international art show for modern and contemporary works, attracting global galleries and artists.	artbasel.com
3	FIAC	Paris, France	Annually in October	75,000	Important French and international contemporary art fair held at the Grand Palais.	fiac.com
4	Frieze Art Fair	London, UK & New York, USA	Annually in October (London)	N/A	Significant contemporary art fair featuring over 170 galleries.	frieze.com
5	Biennale of Sydney	Sydney, Australia	Annually (June 27-September 16)	N/A	Australia's largest contemporary visual arts event, offering free public access to international art.	biennaleofsydney.art
6	Hong Kong	Hong Kong	Annually	>67,000	The largest art event in Asia,	N/A

	Internatio nal Art Fair (ART HK)				showcasing a balanced mix of Eastern and Western galleries.	
7	Whitney Biennial	New York, USA	Every two years	N/A	Focuses on younger, trend-setting artists in America, across various mediums.	whitney.org
8	Echigo-Tsumari Art Triennial	Niigat a Prefec ture, Japan	Every three years (July 29-September 17)	N/A	World's largest outdoor art festival, featuring international artists in a rural setting.	echigo-tsumari.jp
9	Vivid Sydney	Sydne y, Austra lia	Annually	>400,000	Celebrates light, music, and ideas, known for stunning light installations and projections.	vividsydney.co m
10	Harbin Internatio nal Ice and Snow Sculpture Festival	Harbin , China	Annually in January	N/A	One of the world's largest ice and snow festivals, featuring spectacular sculptures.	travelchinaguide .com/cityguides/ heilongjiang/har bin/ice_snow
11	Masterpi ece London	Londo n, UK	Annually in June-July	N/A	Cross-collecting fair offering masterpieces from antique to contemporary across genres.	masterpiecefair. com
12	TEFAF Maastrich t	Maastr icht, Nether lands	Annually in November	70,000	Showcases 7,000 years of art history, from ancient to modern times.	tefaf.com
13	La Biennale Paris	Paris, Franc e	Annually	N/A	Features six millenniums of art, from antiques to modern pieces.	biennaleparis.co m
14	BRAFA Art Fair	Bruss els, Belgiu m	Annually in January-February	66,000	Belgium's major art fair, known for its diverse and high-quality art and antiques.	brafa.art
15	PAD London & Paris	Londo n, UK &	Annually (September 30-October 6	N/A	Focuses on 20th-century art, design, and	pad-fairs.com

		Paris, France	in London)		decorative arts in a refined setting.	
16	Melbourne Art Fair	Melbourne, Australia	Biennially in June	N/A	Represents prestigious	galleries from Australia, New Zealand, and beyond, focusing on contemporary art melbourneartfair.com.au
17	India Art Fair	New Delhi, India	Annually in January-February	N/A		indiaartfair.in
18	ART STAGE Singapore	Singapore	Annually in January	33,200		N/A
19	ArtBo	Bogotá, Colombia	Annually	>35,000		artbo.co
20	arteBA	Buenos Aires, Argentina	Annually in April-May	N/A		arteba.org

Chapter 7

Self-care and Wellbeing for Artists Offline Marketing Strategies

Understanding the Importance of Self-Care

Recognizing the Challenges

The journey of an artist is often marked by a myriad of unique challenges and pressures that can impact their mental, emotional, and physical well-being. From grappling with self-doubt and perfectionism to navigating the unpredictable nature of the creative process, artists face a constant internal and external struggle. The pursuit of artistic excellence can be both exhilarating and exhausting, requiring artists to confront their fears, push beyond their comfort zones, and continually strive for growth. By acknowledging these challenges, artists can begin to understand the importance of prioritizing self-care as an integral part of their artistic practice.

The Connection Between Self-Care and Creativity

Self-care is not just a luxury; it is a fundamental necessity for sustaining creativity, resilience, and overall well-being. Research has shown that engaging in regular self-care practices can enhance cognitive function, boost mood, and alleviate stress, all of which are essential for nurturing creativity. When artists neglect their own needs and push themselves to the brink of burnout, they risk compromising their ability to produce meaningful and impactful work. By incorporating self-care into their daily routines, artists can replenish their creative energy, maintain a healthy work-life balance, and cultivate a sustainable and fulfilling artistic practice.

Prioritizing Physical Well-being

Healthy Habits for Artists

Physical well-being lays the foundation for artistic excellence, yet it is often overlooked in the pursuit of creative endeavors. Emphasizing the importance of nutrition, exercise, and adequate rest is crucial for supporting artists' physical health and energy levels. Incorporating healthy habits into a busy artistic lifestyle can be challenging, but simple strategies such as meal planning, regular exercise breaks, and setting aside time for rest and relaxation can make a significant difference in artists' overall well-bein

Ergonomics and Workspace Optimization

The physical demands of artistic work can take a toll on the body, leading to repetitive strain injuries, eye strain, and other discomforts. Addressing ergonomics and optimizing workspace setup is essential for preventing injuries and promoting long-term physical health. Artists should pay attention to factors such as proper posture, ergonomic seating, adequate lighting, and the organization of their workspace to minimize the risk of physical strain and discomfort.

Cultivating Mental and Emotional Wellness

Managing Stress and Anxiety

The artistic process can be inherently stressful, as artists grapple with self-doubt, creative blocks, and external pressures. Learning to identify and manage stressors is essential for promoting mental well-being. Strategies such as mindfulness, meditation, deep breathing exercises, and creative outlets can help artists reduce anxiety, cultivate resilience, and maintain a sense of calm amid the chaos of artistic life.

Overcoming Creative Blocks

Creative blocks are a common challenge for artists, often leading to frustration, self-doubt, and feelings of inadequacy. Overcoming creative blocks requires patience, persistence, and a willingness to explore new approaches to artistic expression. Artists can employ techniques such as brainstorming exercises, creative prompts, and seeking inspiration from diverse sources to reignite their creativity and break through barriers.

Establishing Work-Life Balance

Setting Boundaries and Priorities

Maintaining a healthy work-life balance is essential for preventing burnout and preserving artists' overall well-being. Setting boundaries between work and personal life, establishing clear priorities, and allocating time for rest, relaxation, and leisure activities outside of art are essential for promoting balance and fulfillment. By honoring their own needs and priorities, artists can ensure that their artistic practice remains sustainable and enjoyable in the long term.

Time Management and Organization

Effective time management and organization are critical skills for artists seeking to maximize productivity and minimize stress. Practical strategies such as creating a daily schedule, setting realistic goals, breaking tasks into manageable chunks, and utilizing productivity tools can help artists stay focused, motivated, and on track with their creative endeavors.

Seeking Support and Community

Building a Support Network

Artists do not have to navigate the challenges of their artistic journey alone. Building a support network of friends, family, mentors, and fellow artists can provide invaluable encouragement, feedback, and perspective during difficult times. By surrounding themselves with a supportive community, artists can find strength, inspiration, and camaraderie to fuel their creative pursuits.

Connecting with the Arts Community

Connecting with the wider arts community is essential for artists seeking to expand their networks, share experiences, and foster a sense of belonging. Opportunities such as workshops, classes, art groups, and online forums provide avenues for artists to connect with like-minded individuals, collaborate on projects, and gain exposure for their work. By actively participating in the arts community, artists can find inspiration, support, and opportunities for growth and collaboration.

Collaborating with Local Businesses

Identify Potential Partners: Look for local businesses that align with your art style or target audience. This can include coffee shops, restaurants, boutiques, and offices.

Offer Mutual Benefits: Propose a collaboration that benefits both parties. Your art can enhance their space, attracting more customers, while providing you with exposure to a broader audience.

Organize Events: Consider partnering with a business to host an art event or exhibition. This can be a great way to draw attention to your work and the business, creating a win-win situation.

Promote the Partnership: Use your and the business's marketing channels to promote the collaboration. This can include social media, newsletters, and local media outlets.

Maintain Relationships: Even after the collaboration ends, maintain the relationship. These connections can lead to future opportunities and continued support

Chapter 8
Sales Channels

Exploring various sales channels is crucial for artists looking to sell their work and reach wider audiences. This chapter covers three primary avenues: selling directly to collectors, working with galleries and agents, and leveraging online sales platforms. Each channel has its unique set of advantages and disadvantages, requiring artists to carefully consider their options based on their goals, preferences, and the stage of their career.

Selling Directly to Collectors

Advantages:

Higher Profit Margins: Selling directly means you keep a larger portion of the sales price since there are no middlemen to take a cut.
Personal Relationships: Direct sales allow you to build personal relationships with your collectors, fostering loyalty and repeat business.

Control Over Pricing: You have complete control over your pricing strategy, allowing for flexibility and adjustments based on your experience and market demand.

Disadvantages:

Time and Effort: Managing sales, marketing, shipping, and customer service can be time-consuming and detract from time spent creating art.

Limited Reach: Without the network and reputation of galleries or agents, reaching new collectors can be challenging.
Market Knowledge: Artists need to become savvy about the art market, which requires research and ongoing education.

Working with Galleries and Agents

Advantages:

Broader Exposure: Galleries and agents have established networks and clientele, providing artists with exposure to a broader audience.

Professional Representation: They handle the business side of selling art, including marketing, sales, negotiations, and logistics, allowing artists to focus on creating.

Career Development: Reputable galleries and agents can offer valuable advice and opportunities for career development, including solo shows and inclusion in prestigious exhibitions.

Disadvantages:

Commission Fees: Galleries and agents typically take a significant percentage of each sale, which can range from 30% to 50%.

Less Control: Artists may have less control over pricing, how their work is marketed, and who it is sold to.

Exclusivity Agreements: Some galleries require exclusivity, limiting artists from selling their work through other channels.

Online Sales Platforms: Pros and Cons

Advantages:

Wide Audience: Online platforms provide access to a global audience, increasing the potential for sales beyond local or national markets.

Ease of Use: Many platforms are user-friendly, offering simple tools for listing and selling art.

Variety of Options: There's a wide range of platforms catering to different types of art and collectors, from prints and crafts to high-end fine art.

Disadvantages:

Competition: The vast number of artists selling online means it can be challenging to stand out and attract attention.

Fees: While less than gallery commissions, online platforms still charge listing fees, transaction fees, or a percentage of sales.

Less Personal Interaction: Selling online means less opportunity to build personal relationships with collectors and receive immediate feedback.

Chapter 9
Customer Relations

In the art business, developing strong customer relations is as crucial as creating compelling art. This chapter focuses on strategies for building relationships with buyers, managing commissions and custom requests, and handling feedback and returns. Effective customer relations can lead to repeat sales, referrals, and a positive reputation in the art community.

Building Relationships with Buyers

Personal Connection: Engage with your buyers personally, whether through direct communication, at shows, or via social media. Share stories behind your art and your process, making them feel connected to your work and you as an artist.

Follow-Up: After a sale, follow up with your buyers to ensure they are satisfied with their purchase and to express your gratitude. This can also be an opportunity to introduce them to your new work or inform them about upcoming shows.

Exclusive Offers: Provide your loyal customers with exclusive offers, previews of new collections, or the opportunity to commission work before you announce it publicly. This makes them feel valued and encourages repeat purchases.

Collect Feedback: Regularly ask for feedback on your work and the buying experience. This not only shows that you value their opinion but also provides you with insights to improve your offerings.

Managing Commissions and Custom Requests

Clear Communication: From the outset, ensure clear communication about the process, timelines, pricing, and any other expectations. This includes drafting a contract that outlines all terms and conditions.

Regular Updates: Keep your clients informed with regular updates throughout the commission process. Share sketches, progress shots, and ask for input at predetermined stages to ensure their satisfaction with the final piece.

Manage Expectations: Be honest about what you can deliver, both in terms of artistic capability and time. It's better to under-promise and over-deliver than to commit to something beyond your reach.

Set Boundaries: Establish clear boundaries regarding revisions, deadlines, and payments. This helps in managing the commission smoothly and professionally.

Handling Feedback and Returns

Positive Feedback: When you receive positive feedback, thank the customer and consider asking them for a testimonial you can use in your marketing materials. Positive feedback can also be shared on social media (with the buyer's permission).

Negative Feedback: Address negative feedback promptly and professionally. Listen to the customer's concerns, and if possible, offer a solution or compromise. Use negative feedback as an opportunity to learn and improve your art or business practices.

Returns Policy: Have a clear returns policy in place and make sure it is communicated to buyers at the point of sale. While returns might be less common for art than other products, a fair policy can reassure potential buyers and build trust.

Resolve Issues Quickly: If a buyer is not satisfied and wishes to return a piece, handle the situation as smoothly and quickly as possible. This can turn a potentially negative experience into a positive one, maintaining a good relationship with the buyer.

Chapter 10
Scaling Your Art Business

Once you've established a foundation for your art business and started making sales, the next step is to consider scaling. Scaling your business can help increase your income and reach without proportionally increasing your workload. This chapter covers strategies for diversifying your product offerings, licensing your art, and exploring passive income opportunities.

Diversifying Your Product Offerings

Prints and Reproductions: Offering high-quality prints or reproductions of your original works can attract buyers with varying budgets and increase the accessibility of your art. Limited edition prints can also add a sense of exclusivity and value.

Merchandise: Expand your product line by applying your art to merchandise such as apparel, stationery, or home decor items. This can appeal to a broader audience and provide more ways for people to engage with your art.

Workshops and Classes: If you enjoy teaching, consider offering workshops or classes. This can be a way to share your skills and passion while also diversifying your income streams.

Digital Products: Create digital products related to your art, such as eBooks, tutorials, or online courses. These can be sold repeatedly without the need for physical inventory.

Licensing Your Art

Understand Licensing: Licensing your art means allowing a company to use your artwork on their products in exchange for a fee. This can significantly expand your reach and provide a steady income stream.

Finding Licensing Opportunities: Research companies that align with your art style and submit your portfolio for consideration. Trade shows and licensing agents can also be valuable resources for finding opportunities.

Negotiating Terms: When negotiating a licensing agreement, consider the scope of use, duration, and compensation. Royalties (a percentage of sales) are common, but flat fees can also be negotiated.

Protecting Your Rights: Ensure that your contract specifies how your art can be used, any exclusivity clauses, and your rights regarding the artwork's future use. It's often advisable to consult with a legal professional when drafting or reviewing contracts.

Exploring Passive Income Opportunities

Print-on-Demand Services: Utilize print-on-demand platforms to sell your art on a variety of products. These services handle production, shipping, and customer service, reducing your workload.

Online Marketplaces: Platforms like Etsy or Society6 can be excellent venues for selling your art and products without the need for a large inventory or handling shipping yourself.

Stock Image Libraries: If you create digital art or photography, consider selling your work through stock image libraries. This can provide ongoing income from your existing work.

Patreon and Membership Sites: Platforms like Patreon allow artists to receive funding directly from their audience in exchange for exclusive content, early access to new work, or other perks.

Chapter 11
Legal and Financial Considerations

For artists, navigating the legal and financial aspects of running an art business is crucial for protecting their work and ensuring their venture's sustainability. This chapter delves into copyrights and intellectual property, contracts and negotiations, and financial planning for artists, offering guidance to help you manage these critical aspects effectively.

Copyrights and Intellectual Property

Understanding Copyright: Copyright automatically protects your original art from the moment of its creation, granting you exclusive rights to use, reproduce, and sell your work. It's essential to understand these rights to prevent unauthorized use and to exploit your art commercially.

Registering Copyright: While not always required, registering your copyright with the relevant government body can offer additional protection and ease the enforcement of your rights. It provides legal evidence of your ownership and can be crucial in infringement cases.

Licensing and Usage Rights: When licensing your art or selling reproductions, clearly define the scope of usage rights. Specify whether the license is exclusive, the duration of the license, and any restrictions on how the art can be used.

Contracts and Negotiations

Importance of Contracts: Always formalize agreements in writing, whether with galleries, agents, or clients commissioning work. Contracts should outline all terms and conditions, including payment, delivery timelines, copyright ownership, and what happens in case of a dispute.

Negotiating Terms: Don't hesitate to negotiate terms that are fair and beneficial to both parties. Understand your worth and the value of your work. Be clear about your expectations and willing to walk away if an agreement does not meet your minimum requirements.

Seek Legal Advice: Consider consulting with a legal professional specializing in art or intellectual property law when drafting or reviewing contracts. This can prevent future legal issues and ensure your interests are adequately protected.

Financial Planning for Artists

Managing Income: Artists often have irregular income streams, making it essential to manage finances carefully. Track all income and expenses, and set aside a portion of sales for taxes and savings.

Budgeting: Create a budget that accounts for art supplies, studio rent, marketing expenses, and personal living costs. Planning can help smooth out financial ups and downs and ensure the sustainability of your art practice.

Taxes and Record-Keeping: Understand your tax obligations, including sales tax on art sold and income tax. Keep detailed records of all transactions, receipts, and expenses, as these are essential for tax purposes and financial analysis.

Diversification: Diversify your income sources to reduce reliance on any single revenue stream. This could include sales of originals and prints, teaching, licensing, and online sales.

Investing in Your Business: Reinvest a portion of your profits back into your business to support its growth. This could involve upgrading equipment, expanding your marketing efforts, or pursuing professional development opportunities.

Chapter 12
Staying Motivated and Productive

For artists, maintaining motivation and productivity is essential for both creative fulfillment and business success. This final chapter addresses overcoming creative blocks, effective time management strategies, the importance of self-care, and concludes with a summary of the key points covered in this guide.

Overcoming Creative Blocks

- **Change Your Environment:** Sometimes, a change of scenery can stimulate creativity. Work in a new location, whether it's a different room, outdoors, or a café.

- **Seek New Inspirations:** Explore other forms of art, read books, or immerse yourself in nature. Inspiration can come from the most unexpected places.

- **Set Small, Achievable Goals:** Breaking down your work into smaller tasks can make it feel more manageable and help you start moving forward.

- **Collaborate with Others:** Working with another artist or creative can bring new ideas and perspectives to your work.

- **Allow Yourself to Create Freely:** Sometimes, the pressure to create something great can hinder creativity. Allow yourself to create without expectations or judgments.

Time Management for Artists

- **Prioritize Your Tasks:** Identify the most critical tasks each day and tackle those first. Understanding what needs your immediate attention can help reduce overwhelm.

- **Set a Schedule:** Having a routine can help you manage your time effectively. Allocate specific times for creating, marketing, administrative tasks, and rest.

- **Use Tools and Technology:** Leverage tools such as calendars, to-do lists, and project management apps to keep track of deadlines and stay organized.

- **Learn to Say No:** Protect your creative time by being selective about the commitments you take on. Saying no to less important tasks allows you to focus on your art.

The Importance of Self-Care

- **Physical Health:** Regular exercise, a healthy diet, and adequate sleep are crucial for maintaining energy levels and creativity.

- **Mental Health:** Engage in activities that reduce stress and promote mental well-being, such as meditation, reading, or spending time with loved ones.

- **Take Regular Breaks:** Short breaks throughout the day can help prevent burnout and keep your creativity flowing.

- **Celebrate Your Achievements:** Take time to acknowledge your accomplishments, no matter how small. This can boost your confidence and motivation.

Chapter 12:

Planning for Your Death as an Artist

Planning for Your Death as an Artist

Planning for your death as an artist is a crucial yet often overlooked aspect of estate planning. It involves making decisions about the disposition of your artwork, legacy, and artistic legacy. Here are some considerations and steps to take in planning for your death as an artist:

Create a Will: The foundation of any estate plan is a legally binding will. In your will, you can specify how you want your assets, including your artwork, to be distributed after your death. Be clear and specific about your wishes regarding your art collection, including who should inherit specific pieces, how they should be divided, and any conditions or restrictions you wish to impose.

Appoint an Executor: Choose a trusted individual to serve as the executor of your estate. The executor will be responsible for carrying out your wishes as outlined in your will, including managing and distributing your art collection according to your instructions. Make sure your executor is familiar with your artistic preferences and understands the importance of preserving your artistic legacy.

Inventory Your Artwork: Create a detailed inventory of your art collection, including descriptions, photographs, provenance, and current market value. Keep this inventory up to date and accessible to your executor and heirs. Consider storing digital copies of your inventory in a secure location, such as a cloud-based storage service, to ensure it can be easily accessed in the event of your death.

Consider a Trust: In addition to a will, you may also consider setting up a trust to manage your art collection after your death. A trust can provide more flexibility and control over how your artwork is distributed and managed, especially if you have specific wishes regarding the use or display of your art. Consult with an estate planning attorney to determine if a trust is the right option for your artistic legacy.

Document Your Artistic Intentions: Write a letter of artistic intent to accompany your will or trust, outlining your artistic philosophy, values, and intentions for your art collection. This letter can provide valuable guidance to your executor and heirs in understanding your wishes and preserving your artistic legacy. Be sure to update this letter periodically to reflect any changes in your artistic vision or preferences.

Consider Donating to Charity: If you have pieces of artwork that hold special significance to you but may not have a clear recipient among your heirs, consider donating them to a charitable organization or museum. Not only can this be a meaningful way to preserve your artistic legacy, but it may also provide tax benefits for your estate. Consult with a tax advisor or estate planning attorney to explore the potential tax implications of charitable donations.

Communicate Your Wishes: Finally, communicate your wishes regarding your art collection to your loved ones and heirs. Discuss your plans openly and honestly with them, and address any questions or concerns they may have. By involving your family and heirs in the planning process, you can help ensure that your wishes are understood and respected after your death.

Planning for your death as an artist is an important part of preserving your artistic legacy and ensuring that your artwork is cared for and appreciated for generations to come. By taking proactive steps to create a comprehensive estate plan, you can provide peace of mind for yourself and your loved ones and leave behind a lasting legacy that reflects your artistic vision and values.

Chapter 13

What to Do When Your Art Doesn't Sell

In the journey of an artist, not all creations find their way into the arms of eager buyers. This chapter is dedicated to those moments when the echo of unsold pieces reverberates louder than the chime of success. It's a guide to navigating these uncharted waters, turning potential despair into a voyage of discovery and growth.

Embracing Reflection and Evolution

The first step on this journey is inward. Ask yourself critical questions about your art. Is your style resonating with your intended audience? Are your marketing efforts reaching the right eyes? Use this time as an opportunity for growth and refinement. Experiment with new techniques, mediums, or subjects that can inject fresh life into your work. Sometimes, a slight change can open up entirely new avenues for exploration and appreciation.

Cultivating Community and Visibility

Art does not exist in a vacuum. Its value and meaning often come to life in the eyes of its beholder. Engage with your local and online communities by offering workshops, participating in art fairs, or simply sharing your process on social media. These interactions can provide invaluable insights into how your work is perceived and what might be missing in your current approach.

Consider collaborating with other artists or creators in different fields. These partnerships can lead to exciting projects that combine diverse talents, offering something unique to the market.

Philanthropy as a Pathway

Your art has the power to make a difference. Donating pieces to charitable causes or local businesses not only serves the community but also puts your work in front of new audiences. It's a gesture that speaks volumes about your character as an artist and can lead to unexpected opportunities through networking and exposure.

Exploring Alternative Avenues

The traditional gallery route is not the only path to success. Online platforms, pop-up exhibitions, and alternative spaces like cafes or community centers can be excellent venues for showcasing your work. Each has its own set of visitors and can attract a different demographic of art lovers.

Moreover, consider the digital art. NFTs (Non-Fungible Tokens) and virtual galleries have opened up new frontiers for artists, allowing digital and traditional creators alike to sell their work in innovative ways.

Building Resilience and Perspective

Finally, it's crucial to cultivate resilience. The art world is subject to trends, tastes, and economic swings that can be beyond your control. What matters is your response to these challenges. View every unsold piece not as a failure but as a stepping stone. Each offers a lesson, a chance to refine your craft, and an opportunity to reassess your strategies.

Remember, the value of your art is not solely defined by its market success. Your creative expression, the joy it brings to you and others, and the journey it represents are equally significant.

In conclusion, when faced with the challenge of unsold art, look beyond the immediate setback. Embrace this phase as a period of growth, exploration, and opportunity. Your art's journey is unique, and so too will be your path to finding its audience. Keep creating, keep sharing, and keep evolving; the next chapter of your artistic journey is yours to write.

Conclusion

Building a successful art business requires more than just talent and creativity. It involves understanding the market, effectively presenting and marketing your art, managing the legal and financial aspects, and, importantly, maintaining your motivation and productivity. This guide has provided strategies and tips to help you navigate these challenges, from identifying your unique selling proposition and leveraging various sales channels to managing customer relations and scaling your business.

Remember, the journey of an artist is both personal and professional. While focusing on the business side, don't lose sight of why you started creating art in the first place. Your passion, creativity, and unique voice are your greatest assets. Stay true to yourself, continually seek growth, and embrace the journey with resilience and optimism.

Reflecting on Your Journey

Reflecting on your artistic journey is crucial for personal and professional growth. It involves looking back at where you started, the progress you've made, and the lessons learned along the way. This reflection can provide valuable insights into your development as an artist and help you identify areas for future growth. Celebrate your achievements, acknowledge the challenges you've overcome, and consider how each experience has shaped your art and your approach to the business of art.

Planning for the Future

Planning for the future is about setting goals and outlining steps to achieve them. Consider where you want to be in one, five, or ten years, both artistically and professionally. Set specific, measurable, achievable, relevant, and time-bound (SMART) goals to guide your journey. Continuously assess and adjust your plans as you grow and as the art market evolves. Stay informed about industry trends, and be open to new opportunities and ways of working. Remember, the path to success is not linear; be prepared to adapt and pivot as necessary.

Art's Indelible Mark on the Artist

The journey into the world of art is often painted as a one-way street, leading many to wonder: Can one ever truly exit the realm of art once they've ventured into its embrace? This chapter delves into the heart of this query, exploring the intricate dance between the innate and the acquired in the realm of artistic expression.

Innate Talent Versus Learned Skill

The inception of an artist's journey is as varied as the art they create. For some, the call to art is a whisper in their soul from the earliest memories, an innate drive to express, create, and communicate through visual means. For others, art unfolds as a learned skill, meticulously cultivated through study, practice, and relentless dedication. This dichotomy raises the question: Is art an intrinsic part of our being, or is it a craft that can be picked up and set aside at will?

Art as an Integral Part of Self

For many artists, the act of creating is not merely a pursuit or a profession but an essential aspect of their identity. It becomes a lens through which they view the world, a fundamental mode of understanding and interacting with their surroundings. In this light, art is not something one does but something one is. It's woven into the fabric of their being, making the notion of completely abandoning it akin to forsaking a part of oneself.

Shifting Mediums and Modalities

The journey of an artist is seldom linear. It's punctuated by periods of exploration, transformation, and sometimes, significant shifts in medium or style. These evolutions can sometimes feel like leaving one art form for another, yet they often represent the artist's underlying quest for growth and self-expression. This fluidity underscores the idea that while one may diverge from their initial path, the essence of being an artist remains.

Stepping Away from Art

Yet, it is undeniable that some individuals may choose to step away from art as a central pursuit. This decision can be driven by various factors, from career changes to life's unpredictable demands. However, even in these transitions, the impact of art remains. The skills honed, the way artists observe the world, and their capacity for creative thinking endure, influencing their approaches to new challenges and ventures.

Beyond the Canvas

Ultimately, whether art is an inborn trait or a skill honed over time, its impact on the individual is profound and enduring. The principles of composition, balance, and contrast; the sensitivity to beauty and emotion; the ability to convey complex ideas through imagery—these are gifts that persist, regardless of whether one continues to create art in a traditional sense.

The Unbreakable Bond

In contemplating the question of exiting the world of art, it becomes evident that art is not merely a profession or a hobby but a way of seeing and being in the world. It leaves an indelible mark on the soul that transcends the physical act of creating. So, while one may physically move away from making art, the essence of what it means to be an artist—a seeker, a dreamer, a creator—remains an integral part of one's identity, forever shaping their view of the world and their place within it.

Appendices

Online Platforms and Resources for Artists

Website	Description
Artsy (artsy.net)	Comprehensive platform connecting collectors with galleries, auctions, and artists worldwide, offering a wide range of artworks and insights into art market trends.
Saatchi Art (saatchiart.com)	Online gallery showcasing original artworks by emerging and established artists, providing a diverse selection of artworks for collectors to browse and purchase directly.
Artfinder (artfinder.com)	Global marketplace for original artwork, featuring paintings, sculptures, prints, and photography from artists worldwide, offering a platform for artists to showcase their work.
Artspace (artspace.com)	Online marketplace featuring limited edition prints, curated collections, and exclusive artworks by leading contemporary artists, catering to seasoned collectors and buyers.
1stdibs (1stdibs.com)	Luxury online marketplace specializing in fine art, antiques, and collectibles, offering a curated selection of artworks from top galleries, dealers, and artists.
Etsy (etsy.com)	Online marketplace hosting a vibrant community of artists selling original artwork, prints, and illustrations alongside handmade crafts and vintage goods.
Artplode (artplode.com)	Online art gallery enabling artists to sell artwork directly to buyers without commission fees, providing a transparent platform for showcasing and selling artwork.
Artforum (artforum.com)	Leading art magazine and online platform offering news, reviews, and features on contemporary art and culture, serving as a valuable resource for artists and enthusiasts.
ArtStation (artstation.com)	Community-driven platform focusing on digital art, providing artists with a space to showcase portfolios, connect with professionals, and explore career opportunities.

Redbubble (redbubble.com)	Online marketplace featuring artwork and designs from independent artists, printed on various products such as art prints, clothing, and home decor.
Art Basel (artbasel.com)	Leading international art fair with editions in Basel, Miami Beach, and Hong Kong, providing information about upcoming fairs, galleries, and artworks showcased at the events.
Artnet (artnet.com)	Comprehensive platform offering auction results, art market news, and a database of artworks, artists, and galleries, serving as a valuable resource for collectors and dealers.
Art.sy (artsy.net)	Online platform using artificial intelligence to recommend artworks to users based on their preferences, featuring a vast collection from galleries, museums, and artists.
Artprice (artprice.com)	Leading art market database providing pricing information, auction results, and analytics for artworks and artists, offering insights for collectors and investors.
ArtistsNetwork (artistsnetwork.com)	Community-driven platform offering resources, tutorials, and inspiration for artists working in various mediums, including painting, drawing, and mixed media.
DeviantArt (deviantart.com)	Social media platform and online community for artists to share artwork, receive feedback, and connect with other artists, fostering a vibrant global community of creators.
Society6 (society6.com)	Online marketplace featuring artwork and designs from independent artists, printed on various products such as art prints, clothing, and home decor.
UGallery (ugallery.com)	Online gallery showcasing original artwork by emerging and established artists, offering curated collections for collectors to browse and purchase.
The Art Newspaper (theartnewspaper.com)	Leading publication covering news, events, and developments in the art world, providing articles, reviews, and analysis for artists, collectors, and enthusiasts.
ArtRabbit (artrabbit.com)	Platform providing information about art exhibitions, events, and openings worldwide, serving as a valuable resource for discovering new artists and artworks.
Artists' Union England (artistsunionengland.org.uk)	Trade union representing visual and applied artists in England, offering resources, advocacy, and support for artists navigating the art world.
Art UK (artuk.org)	Digital platform providing access to artworks from public collections across the UK, offering a comprehensive database for researching British art history and culture.
ArtFacts (artfacts.net)	Online database offering information about artists, galleries, exhibitions, and art fairs worldwide, providing insights for collectors and enthusiasts.
Axisweb (axisweb.org)	Platform showcasing contemporary artists based in the UK, offering profiles, portfolios, and networking opportunities for artists alongside resources for professional development.

Art in America (artinamericamagazine.com)	Leading art magazine covering news, reviews, and features on contemporary art and culture, providing articles and analysis for artists and enthusiasts.
The Art Story (theartstory.org)	Online resource offering information about art movements, styles, and artists throughout history, providing timelines and articles to understand the evolution of art over time.
The Smithsonian American Art Museum (americanart.si.edu)	Website offering access to the vast collection of American artwork, including paintings, sculpture, photography, and decorative arts, providing resources for research and education.

Art Auction Houses

Auction House	Website	Description
Sotheby's	sothebys.com	Prestigious auction house specializing in fine art, jewelry, antiques, and collectibles.
Christie's	christies.com	International auction house is known for sales of fine art, decorative arts, jewelry, and rare collectibles.
Phillips	phillips.com	Leading auction house specializing in contemporary art, modern art, design, and photography.
Bonhams	bonhams.com	Global auction house offering sales in fine art, antiques, motorcars, and jewelry.
Heritage Auctions	ha.com	One of the largest auction houses with sales in fine art, rare books, coins, and sports memorabilia.
Julien's Auctions	juliensauctions.com	Specializes in celebrity memorabilia, entertainment artifacts, and pop culture collectibles.
Doyle	doyle.com	New York-based auction house known for sales of fine art, jewellery, furniture, and decorative arts.
Swann Auction Galleries	swanngalleries.com	Leading auction house specializing in rare and vintage books, prints, photographs, and maps.
Freeman's Auction	freemansauction.com	America's oldest auction house offering sales in fine art, jewelry, furniture, and decorative arts.
Leslie Hindman Auctioneers	lesliehindman.com	Conducts auctions of fine art, jewelry, furniture, and decorative arts across the United States.
Skinner Auctioneers	skinnerinc.com	Specializes in fine art, antiques, jewelry, and decorative arts, with sales held in Massachusetts.
Wright Auction House	wrightauction.com	Focuses on modern and contemporary design, offering sales of furniture, decorative arts, and collectible objects.
Rago Auctions	ragoarts.com	Specializes in 20th-century design, offering sales

		of furniture, ceramics, glass, and fine art.
Boningtons Auctioneers	boningtons.com	Conducts auctions of fine art, antiques, and collectibles in the United Kingdom.
Paddle8	paddle8.com	Online auction house specializing in contemporary art, photography, and collectibles.
Gurr Johns	gurrjohns.com	Provides valuation and advisory services for fine art, jewelry, and collectibles.
Bonhams & Butterfields	bonhams.com	Conducts auctions of fine art, antiques, and collectibles in California.
Capo Auction	capoauctionnyc.com	Specializes in Asian art, offering sales of Chinese ceramics, jade, paintings, and collectibles.
Morton Auctioneers	mortonauctioneers.com	Conducts auctions of fine art, antiques, and collectibles in Houston, Texas.
Hindman Auctions	hindmanauctions.com	Offers sales in fine art, decorative arts, jewelry, and rare collectibles across multiple locations.

Art Museums

Below are a list of well-known art museums

Museum	Location	Website	Description
Louvre Museum	Paris, France	louvre.fr	The Louvre is one of the world's largest and most visited museums, housing an extensive collection of art and artifacts spanning thousands of years.
Museum of Modern Art (MoMA)	New York City, USA	moma.org	MoMA is a leading institution dedicated to modern and contemporary art, featuring a diverse collection of paintings, sculptures, and multimedia installations.
Hermitage Museum	Saint Petersburg, Russia	hermitagemuseum.org	The Hermitage is one of the largest and oldest museums in the world, known for its vast collection of art and cultural treasures from around the globe.
British Museum	London, England	britishmuseum.org	The British Museum houses a comprehensive collection of art and artifacts representing the history and cultures of civilizations spanning thousands of years.
National Gallery	London, England	nationalgallery.org.uk	The National Gallery features a rich collection of European paintings from the 13th to the 19th centuries, including works by renowned artists such as Leonardo da Vinci and Vincent van Gogh.
Rijksmuseum	Amsterdam, Netherlands	rijksmuseum.nl	The Rijksmuseum is the national museum of the Netherlands, showcasing Dutch art and history, including masterpieces by Rembrandt, Vermeer, and Van Gogh.
Metropolitan Museum of Art (The Met)	New York City, USA	metmuseum.org	The Met is one of the largest and most prestigious art museums in the world, featuring an extensive collection of artworks

			spanning various cultures and time periods.
Uffizi Gallery	Florence, Italy	uffizi.it	The Uffizi Gallery is renowned for its collection of Renaissance masterpieces, including works by Michelangelo, Botticelli, and Raphael, among others.
Prado Museum	Madrid, Spain	museodelprado.es	The Prado Museum houses one of the finest collections of European art, with a focus on Spanish masterpieces by artists such as Velázquez, Goya, and El Greco.
Tate Modern	London, England	tate.org.uk	Tate Modern is a renowned contemporary art museum housed in a former power station, featuring a diverse collection of modern and contemporary artworks.
National Museum of China	Beijing, China	chnmuseum.cn	The National Museum of China is the largest museum in the country, showcasing China's rich cultural heritage through its vast collection of artifacts and artworks.
Musée d'Orsay	Paris, France	musee-orsay.fr	Musée d'Orsay is renowned for its collection of Impressionist and Post-Impressionist masterpieces by artists such as Monet, Van Gogh, and Renoir.
Vatican Museums	Vatican City	museivaticani.va	The Vatican Museums house an extensive collection of art and artifacts amassed by the Catholic Church over the centuries, including the Sistine Chapel ceiling painted by Michelangelo.
Art Institute of Chicago	Chicago, USA	artic.edu	The Art Institute of Chicago is one of the oldest and largest art museums in the United States, featuring a vast collection of artworks from around the world.
Guggenheim Museum	New York City, USA	guggenheim.org	The Guggenheim Museum is renowned for its distinctive Frank Lloyd Wright-designed building and its collection of modern and contemporary art.
National Gallery of Art	Washington D.C., USA	nga.gov	The National Gallery of Art houses a diverse collection of European and American artworks, spanning centuries and encompassing a wide range of artistic styles.
State Hermitage Museum	Saint Petersburg, Russia	hermitagemuseum.org	The State Hermitage Museum is one of the largest and most prestigious museums in the world, known for its vast collection of art and cultural artifacts.
Getty Center	Los Angeles, USA	getty.edu	The Getty Center is renowned for its extensive collection of European and American art, housed in a stunning Richard Meier-designed campus overlooking Los Angeles.
Museum of Fine Arts	Boston, USA	mfa.org	The Museum of Fine Arts, Boston, is one of the most comprehensive art museums in the world, featuring a diverse collection of artworks from various cultures and time periods.
National Palace	Taipei,	npm.gov.tw	The National Palace Museum in Taipei houses

Museum	Taiwan		one of the largest collections of Chinese art and artifacts in the world, spanning thousands of years of history.

Quality Art Brands

Brand	Website	Description
Winsor & Newton	winsornewton.com	Renowned manufacturer of paints, brushes, and other art materials known for reliability.
Prismacolor	prismacolor.com	Premium-quality colored pencils, markers, and drawing tools favored by artists.
Faber-Castell	fabercastell.com	Wide range of pencils, pens, and other art supplies known for durability and precision.
Copic	copicmarker.com	High-quality markers and inks favored by illustrators and designers for blending capabilities.
Derwent	derwentart.com	Diverse range of pencils, pens, and accessories for drawing, sketching, and coloring.
Liquitex	liquitex.com	Comprehensive range of acrylic paints and mediums known for high pigment load and durability.
Golden Artist Colors	goldenpaints.com	Professional-grade acrylic paints, mediums, and grounds known for exceptional quality.
Holbein	holbeinartistmaterials.com	Premium-quality paints, pigments, and accessories for artists known for rich colors.
Gamblin	gamblincolors.com	Manufacturer of oil paints, mediums, and varnishes known for quality and sustainability.
Daniel Smith	danielsmith.com	Professional-grade watercolors, oil paints, and acrylics known for intense pigments

		and lightfastness.
Moleskine	moleskine.com	High-quality sketchbooks, notebooks, and planners favored by artists and writers.
Strathmore	strathmoreartist.com	Artist papers including sketchbooks, drawing pads, and watercolor pads known for quality.
Arches	arches-papers.com	Fine art papers for watercolor, printmaking, and drawing known for exceptional quality.
Daler-Rowney	daler-rowney.com	Wide range of artist materials including paints, brushes, and canvases known for quality.
Staedtler	staedtler.com	Drawing and writing instruments including pencils, pens, and markers known for precision.
Caran d'Ache	carandache.com	Colored pencils, watercolor pencils, and drawing materials known for exceptional color brilliance.
Mont Marte	montmarte.net	Art supplies including paints, brushes, and canvases known for affordability and quality.
Pebeo	pebeo.com	Paints, inks, and mediums known for innovative formulations and vibrant colors.
Sakura	sakuraofamerica.com	Pens, markers, and drawing tools known for archival quality and smooth performance.
Winsor & Newton Cotman	winsornewton.com	Affordable watercolor paints and brushes known for quality and color brilliance.